InterActions
small group series

Experiencing
the Joy of
Serving

LOVE IN
ACTION

Interactions Small Group Series

Authenticity: Being Honest with God and Others
Character: Reclaiming Six Endangered Qualities
Commitment: Developing Deeper Devotion to Christ
Community: Building Relationships within God's Family
Essential Christianity: Practical Steps for Spiritual Growth
Fruit of the Spirit: Living the Supernatural Life
Getting a Grip: Finding Balance in Your Daily Life
Jesus: Seeing Him More Clearly
Lessons on Love: Building Deeper Relationships
Living in God's Power: Finding God's Strength for Life's Challenges
Love in Action: Experiencing the Joy of Serving
Marriage: Building Real Intimacy
Meeting God: Psalms for the Highs and Lows of Life
New Identity: Discovering Who You Are in Christ
Parenting: How to Raise Spiritually Healthy Kids
Prayer: Opening Your Heart to God
Reaching Out: Sharing God's Love Naturally
The Real Deal: Discover the Rewards of Authentic Relationships
Significance: Understanding God's Purpose for Your Life
Transformation: Letting God Change You from the Inside Out

InterActions
small group series

Experiencing
the Joy of
Serving

LOVE IN ACTION

Previously published as *Serving Lessons*

BILL HYBELS
WITH KEVIN AND SHERRY HARNEY

ZONDERVAN™

GRAND RAPIDS, MICHIGAN 49530 USA

WILLOW
Willow Creek Resources

Love in Action
Copyright © 1998 by Willow Creek Association
Previously published as *Serving Lessons*

Requests for information should be addressed to:

Zondervan, *Grand Rapids, Michigan 49530*

ISBN-10: 0-310-26607-6
ISBN-13: 978-0-310-26607-5

Interior design by Rick Devon and Michelle Espinoza

Printed in the United States of America

05 06 07 08 09 10 11 12 /❖ DCI/ 10 9 8 7 6 5 4 3 2 1

CONTENTS

INTERACTIONS

In 1992, Willow Creek Community Church, in partnership with Zondervan and the Willow Creek Association, released a curriculum for small groups entitled the Walking with God series. In just three years, almost a half million copies of these small group study guides were being used in churches around the world. The phenomenal response to this curriculum affirmed the need for relevant and biblical small group materials.

At the writing of this curriculum, there are nearly 3,000 small groups meeting regularly within the structure of Willow Creek Community Church. We believe this number will increase as we continue to place a central value on small groups. Many other churches throughout the world are growing in their commitment to small group ministries as well, so the need for resources is increasing.

In response to this great need, the Interactions small group series has been developed. Willow Creek Association and Zondervan have joined together to create a whole new approach to small group materials. These discussion guides are meant to challenge group members to a deeper level of sharing, create lines of accountability, move followers of Christ into action, and help group members become fully devoted followers of Christ.

SUGGESTIONS FOR INDIVIDUAL STUDY

1. Begin each session with prayer. Ask God to help you understand the passage and to apply it to your life.
2. A good modern translation, such as the New International Version, the New American Standard Bible, or the New Revised Standard Version, will give you the most help. Questions in this guide are based on the New International Version.
3. Read and reread the passage(s). You must know what the passage says before you can understand what it means and how it applies to you.
4. Write your answers in the spaces provided in the study guide. This will help you to express clearly your understanding of the passage.
5. Keep a Bible dictionary handy. Use it to look up unfamiliar words, names, or places.

SUGGESTIONS FOR GROUP STUDY

1. Come to the session prepared. Careful preparation will greatly enrich your time in group discussion.
2. Be willing to join in the discussion. The leader of the group will not be lecturing but will encourage people to discuss what they have learned in the passage. Plan to share what God has taught you in your individual study.
3. Stick to the passage being studied. Base your answers on the verses being discussed rather than on outside authorities such as commentaries or your favorite author or speaker.
4. Try to be sensitive to the other members of the group. Listen attentively when they speak, and be affirming whenever you can. This will encourage more hesitant members of the group to participate.
5. Be careful not to dominate the discussion. By all means participate, but allow others to have equal time.
6. If you are the discussion leader, you will find additional suggestions and helpful ideas in the Leader's Notes.

ADDITIONAL RESOURCES AND TEACHING MATERIALS

At the end of this study guide you will find a collection of resources and teaching materials to help you in your growth as a follower of Christ. You will also find resources that will help your church develop and build fully devoted followers of Christ.

INTRODUCTION:
LOVE IN ACTION

A columnist from Florida observed some time ago that our world is made up of all kinds of people. He noted, for instance, that there are dog people and there are cat people. There are swimming-pool people, and there are beach people. There are morning people, and there are evening people. There are coffee people and tea people. There are Ice Capade people and hockey people. There are tennis people and golf people. There are breakfast people and people who can't quite remember what breakfast is. There are sailboat people and powerboat people. There are suitcase people and garment bag people. I think you get the idea; our world is full of all different kinds of people. There is a kaleidoscopic variety of interests, values, and idiosyncrasies among human beings.

But among all this incredible diversity, all of us are strangely similar in one area of interest. Do you know what it is?

Self-interest!

Self-interest is one of the few things that unifies us as a human race. It is the kind of interest that makes four-way intersections so perilous. Four-way stops unmask the universal dark side of the human animal. "Me first." "No, me first." "I'll show you." And this same self-interest makes the last piece of apple pie become the precipitator of World War III around the kitchen table. I think you know what I am talking about.

If we are going to be honest with each other and God, we have to admit that all of us struggle with old-fashioned, grassroots self-centeredness. It takes a tremendous toll on our quality of life at work, in our marriage relationships, in the parenting process, and with friendships. It even affects the life of a church. The "me-first" mind-set filters every activity, decision, opportunity, and commitment on the basis of what it will mean for ourselves above all else. Will it give *me* pleasure? Will it forward *my* concerns? Will it increase *my* net worth? Will it make *me* look good? Will it make *me* feel good? If so, let's go. If not, I'll pass. I would guess that self-centeredness has a greater grip on our thoughts, decisions, values, and relationships than we could ever imagine.

Our generation has been called the most self-centered culture in modern history—the "me" generation. But the "me-first" mind-set is not a new phenomenon. In fact, it is as old as mankind itself, and clearly traceable back to the days of Adam and Eve. It is a problem that was exposed, confronted, and fiercely attacked by none other than the Son of God Himself. Mark 10:45 says, "For even the Son of Man did not come to be served, but to serve, and to give his life as a ransom for many."

In the midst of a "me-first" world, followers of Christ are called to be servants. This flies in the face of almost everything we have known; however, it is the call of God on the life of every person who discovers the love of God given through Jesus. The pursuit of a life of service is not easy, but it is a journey like no other.

Bill Hybels

EXPOSING THE "ME-FIRST" MIND-SET

THE BIG PICTURE

What is the message of our culture today? What is the common thread of thought that weaves its way through almost everything we do? What is the core value that drives and guides the lives of most people? All we have to do is walk around in our society and we will begin to develop this particular mind-set almost by osmosis.

It is a "me-first" mind-set. This mind-set says indulge yourself, fulfill your desires, satiate your appetites, pursue pleasure, take off all restraints. As much as we might want to pretend that this value system died in the eighties, let's be honest: it is alive and still thriving.

With this mind-set comes an elusive promise: If you seek first your own good and satisfy your own desires, then you will be happy. In print, on television, and in the movies, over and over we hear the lie. The road to contentment, satisfaction, fulfillment, and true joy is marked with a street sign flashing "Me First."

The truth is, this perverted and backward view of life is leading to modern day madness. Our society is on the verge of internal collapse. Escapism is running rampant. Perversion of sexuality has become almost common fare. Unwanted pregnancies by the thousands are being terminated every day. Men and women walk away from their commitment to spouse, children, job, and many other life responsibilities with growing ease. People are pathologically self-centered and ignore the needs of others. The "me-first" mind-set is controlling many lives, even the lives of those who call themselves followers of Christ.

A WIDE ANGLE VIEW

1 What are some signs that the "me-first" mind-set is alive and thriving in *one* of these areas:

- In the marketplace
- In the church
- In families
- In your country
- In the media

A BIBLICAL PORTRAIT

Read Mark 8:31–38

2 What do you learn about Jesus' view of Himself in this passage?

What do you learn about Jesus' view of His followers?

3 Jesus was clear about His commitment to suffer and die for His followers. Why do you think Peter tried to stand in the way of Jesus' plan?

Why was Jesus' response to Peter's resistance so severe?

SHARPENING THE FOCUS

Read Snapshot "Grappling with Greatness"

GRAPPLING WITH GREATNESS

Jesus tried again and again to expose and attack self-centeredness in His disciples. He wanted them to have a "Father-first" mind-set but often saw their "me-first" mind-set prevailing. Once, while walking down a road toward a city called Capernaum, some of Jesus' followers were debating among themselves which of them was the greatest. In the gospel of Mark we read these words: "They came to Capernaum. When he was in the house, he asked them, 'What were you arguing about on the road?' But they kept quiet because on the way they had argued about who was the greatest" (Mark 9:33–34).

Jesus had just preached a powerful sermon on servanthood, yet the disciples still did not get the point. In an effort to drive the point home even more clearly, Jesus added: "If anyone wants to be first, he must be the very last, and the servant of all" (Mark 9:35). While the disciples wanted a *position of greatness*, Jesus called them to have a *passion for service*.

---

4 What are some of the warning signs and symptoms you see in your life when you are striving for a "position of greatness"?

What would your life look like if you developed a greater passion for service?

Read Snapshot "Indiscriminate Service"

INDISCRIMINATE SERVICE

Jesus calls us to serve indiscriminately. In Mark 10:13 people began bringing little children to Jesus so He would touch them. The disciples got angry and rebuked the crowds. In their minds, these little children were not important enough to waste Jesus' time. After all, children weren't powerful people, and they had no influence or authority, so Jesus shouldn't give them the time of day.

When Jesus realized what was going on, He became angry. He insisted that the disciples permit the little ones to come to Him. He did not want them to hinder or get in the way of the children. He wanted His disciples, and the whole world, to know that the kingdom of God belonged to such as these.

In receiving the little children, Jesus was calling His followers to turn from arrogance to humility, to stop serving only those who could return the favor and to begin serving indiscriminately. Jesus was saying, "Change your mind-set. Get off the 'me-first' bandwagon and adopt a 'Father-first' look at life."

---

5 What might our service look like when we approach it with *one* of the following attitudes:

- I will serve those who have influence, power, or who can repay my kindness.
- I will serve those who are like me . . . those whom I understand and around whom I feel comfortable.
- I will serve those with needs, regardless of their status, age, or position in life.

6 Who were some of the people Jesus served when He walked on this earth?

How does His example influence your view of whom you should serve?

Read Snapshot "I Want to Be First"

I WANT TO BE FIRST

Again and again Jesus drove the message home: Don't be consumed with a "me-first" mind-set. You might think that after all of Jesus' clear teaching on the topic the disciples would have gotten the point. But it had still not soaked in. In Mark 10:35–37, James and John approached Jesus and made a "little" request. They said, "Teacher, we want you to do for us *whatever we ask*." When Jesus asked them what they wanted, James and John replied, "Let one of us sit at your right and the other at your left in your glory." They wanted the two most prominent and powerful positions in the universe next to Jesus!

7 How does our culture encourage and praise those who strive for positions of power and prominence?

How does our society treat those who don't compete for first place?

What implications does this have for the Christian who is committed to following Christ's example?

8

Describe one area in your life in which you are presently working to gain a position of power and prominence.

How do these efforts look in light of Christ's teachings on the "me-first" mind-set?

PUTTING YOURSELF IN THE PICTURE

AN HONEST LOOK AT MY MIND-SET

Take time in the coming week to reflect on where you see a "me-first" mind-set in your life. Make note of any indications of a "me-first" approach to life in the following areas:

- In your home
- In your workplace
- In your friendships
- In your church life
- In your social settings
- In other areas

FILLING YOUR MIND WITH A NEW VIEW

Often our thought patterns are formed by what we feed into our minds. Take time in the coming week to memorize the passage below and to reflect on what it means. How does this truth from the lips of Jesus impact the way you see yourself and others?

Jesus called them together and said, "You know that those who are regarded as rulers of the Gentiles lord it over them, and their high officials exercise authority over them. Not so with you. Instead, whoever wants to become great among you must be your servant, and whoever wants to be first must be slave of all. For even the Son of Man did not come to be served, but to serve, and to give his life as a ransom for many" (Mark 10:42–45).

BREAKING THE BACK OF SELF-CENTEREDNESS

REFLECTIONS FROM SESSION 1

1. If you took time since your last group meeting to evaluate where you have a "me-first" mind-set in your life, what did you discover?
2. If you memorized Mark 10:42–45, would you be willing to recite it for your group? How has meditating on this passage impacted your understanding of Christian service?

THE BIG PICTURE

Over the course of three years, Jesus' followers heard many sermons calling them to change from a "me-first" mind-set to a "Father-first" mind-set. They had seen Jesus model this lifestyle over and over again. Yet even as Jesus drew near the end of His earthly ministry, His disciples had still not gotten the point. In a final effort to communicate the critical importance of breaking the back of self-centeredness, Jesus gave them one more lesson.

Jesus gathered with His disciples in an upper room to celebrate one final meal together before He would die on the cross. It is important to know that the cultural custom of the day involved a host providing a servant at the door of any dinner party to wash the feet of the guests. Remember, in those days people walked with sandals down dusty roads and reclined at low tables—a foot to eighteen inches above the ground—while eating. That meant their feet would be dangerously near the next person's face. Having a foot washer greet guests at the door was standard practice, much like we would have someone greet visitors and offer to take their coat and hang it up.

Imagine you can see everything in the room, but no one in the room can see you. You stand, unnoticed, and watch the events of the Last Supper. Here come the twelve with Jesus, climbing the stairs. The first disciple walks in the door, looks for the foot-washing servant and notices he is not there. Does he wash his own feet? Does he take off his garment and become a rank-and-file servant and wash everyone else's feet? Look at his eyes. He is saying, "Not me. I'm a disciple of the great teacher Jesus. I don't identify with the rank and file." So he hurries to the table to get a good spot. The second disciple comes in. Realizing that the first guy refused to be a servant, he comes to the same conclusion. He too goes in and looks for a good spot at the table. Each disciple does the same thing. They all file in. They all go right past the water basin to recline at the table, making themselves comfortable as they stick their dirty feet in each other's faces.

Finally Jesus and His twelve followers are all at the table. Jesus looks at the water. He looks at the filthy feet of the disciples. You can see it in His eyes. Unbelievable! Three years, sermon after sermon after sermon, illustration after illustration, confrontation after confrontation, and not one of them is willing to serve his brothers. And even more heartbreaking, not one of them was humble enough to serve even Jesus.

After giving every chance for one of them to take the role of a servant, Jesus gets up from the table. No one knows where He is going or what He is about to do. Jesus quietly walks to the water basin and begins to remove His outer garment. He carefully picks up the servant's towel and tucks it in His belt, exactly the way a common servant would. Then He pours the water into the basin and kneels down at the feet of one of His followers.

The disciples' faces show disbelief, then embarrassment. Jesus begins to wash the filthy feet of His followers. What do you see in their eyes? Agony, regret, maybe tears. What are they thinking? "What is the matter with me? I'm finally beginning to see it. My whole world revolves around me. How could I have done this? It is one thing that I wasn't humble enough to wash the brothers' feet, but I didn't even think to wash my Savior's feet."

Jesus finishes washing all of their feet, takes off the towel, folds it, puts on His robe, and comes back to recline at the table. Then He takes a piece of bread and He breaks it and says, "This is my body which is broken for you." Next, He takes a cup and He pours it out saying, "This is my blood. I pour it out for you." In doing so, He lets them know that there will be one more act of service: the giving of His life.

Jesus words to His followers were clear:

You call me "Teacher" and "Lord," and rightly so, for that is what I am. Now that I, your Lord and Teacher, have washed your feet, you also should wash one another's feet. I have set you an example that you should do as I have done for you. (John 13:13–15)

A WIDE ANGLE VIEW

1 In Jesus' day, washing feet was one of the lowest forms of service. What are some of the acts of service in our culture today that many people avoid doing because they feel "above it"?

What is one specific task, chore, or act of service that you avoid, hoping someone else will do it?

A BIBLICAL PORTRAIT

Read Luke 19:1–10

2 Zacchaeus was a self-centered, greedy businessman. Discuss the metamorphosis that occurred in his life.

What caused the change within Zacchaeus?

What were the outward signs of the inner change Zacchaeus experienced?

3 *What part did Jesus play in this life-changing encounter?*

What part did Zacchaeus have in the transformation of his life?

How do you see the partnership of God and man in this process of change?

SHARPENING THE FOCUS

Read Snapshot "Meeting Jesus"

MEETING JESUS

Zacchaeus discovered a powerful truth: The first blow in destroying the power of self-centeredness in our lives is meeting Jesus face-to-face. When a person receives salvation by grace, is adopted into God's family, and realizes the promise of eternal life, something dramatic happens. When a person bows before Christ and realizes he or she could never merit eternal life, but that God's love has made a way, the back of self-centeredness receives a powerful blow.

Isn't that what happened to the apostle Paul? He was consumed with his own agenda, resisting God and charting his own course. Then, out of the clear blue sky, when he least expected it, he was confronted by the living Christ. Paul asked, "Who is it?" and Jesus introduced Himself. Paul's response was to ask, "What do you want me to do?" Do you see the shift? Not my agenda anymore, not me first, not self-centeredness, but a willingness to follow God's plan.

4 Describe when you first met Jesus—when He first became real to you.

How did this encounter impact the way you view yourself and others?

Read Snapshot "Renewing Our Minds"

RENEWING OUR MINDS

A second way God defeats the enemy of self-centeredness is by the renewing of our minds. In Philippians 2:3–4 the apostle Paul talks about a new mind-set. He writes, "Do nothing out of selfish ambition or vain conceit, but in humility consider others better than yourselves. Each of you should look not only to your own interests, but also to the interests of others." What a message! After this invitation, Paul holds up Jesus as the ultimate example of this kind of service-centered mind-set.

Too much servanthood is emotionally inspired these days. For example, when believers hear a series of messages on servanthood, they might get on a two-week service "high." They are running on emotional adrenaline. But what happens after the high wears off? They go back to the "me-first" mind-set. Emotional energy burns low, the inspiration fades, and it's back to a self-centered lifestyle. Jesus was trying to instill in His followers a crisp, intellectual understanding of the futility of the "me-first" mind-set and the brilliance of the servant mind-set. He was saying to His followers, "Think about it. Self-indulgence is a dead-end road. Look around and you will see example after example of shattered lives resulting from a 'me-first' mind-set." Jesus wants His followers to know that true fulfillment comes only through faithful service to God and humble service to others. This is the only sensible way to live.

5 Describe a classic case of someone you have seen pursuing a "me-first" mind-set.

What were some of the consequences they reaped because of this lifestyle?

6

Describe a time in your life when you had to face the hard consequences of living with a "me-first" mind-set.

How does remembering this experience deepen your desire to have a service-centered mind-set?

Read Snapshot "Examples of Servanthood"

EXAMPLES OF SERVANTHOOD

A third way God breaks the back of self-centeredness in the lives of His people is to surround them with shining examples of servanthood. In the beginning of this session you saw a picture of Jesus taking off His outer robe, tucking a towel in His belt, and washing the feet of His disciples. Jesus wanted to firmly imbed a picture in their minds of Himself, the Son of God, humbly serving. After Jesus' death, the disciples had many memories of their Savior. I have to believe that two of the most vivid ones were of Jesus washing their feet and of their Savior hanging on the cross, dying for their sins. We need to live with these same images burned in our minds.

Along with Christ as our ultimate example, each of us is usually exposed to a few faithful servants who model a level of self-sacrifice that inspires us to greater growth in serving. You see, servanthood is contagious. When you are continually surrounded by service-centered people, you tend to become rather service-centered yourself. You catch the vision. You are inspired to serve with joy.

7

Describe someone in your life who lives with a clear servant's mind-set.

What are the results of this person's servant lifestyle?

How has this person inspired you to be more of a servant?

PUTTING YOURSELF IN THE PICTURE

THE MIND OF CHRIST

The apostle Paul calls us to adopt the mind-set of Jesus Christ. Take time in the coming week to memorize Philippians 2:1–5. Pray through this passage daily and ask God to help you have the heart and mind of Christ.

If you have any encouragement from being united with Christ, if any comfort from his love, if any fellowship with the Spirit, if any tenderness and compassion, then make my joy complete by being like-minded, having the same love, being one in spirit and purpose. Do nothing out of selfish ambition or vain conceit, but in humility consider others better than yourselves. Each of you should look not only to your own interests, but also to the interests of others. Your attitude should be the same as that of Christ Jesus.

THANKS FOR YOUR EXAMPLE

We have all had people in our lives who were examples of humble, Christ-like servanthood. Take time in the coming week to contact one of these people in your life. You may want to write a note, or call him on the telephone, or maybe take her out to lunch. However you choose to do it, thank that person for his servant example and let him know how God has inspired and challenged you through his life.

GIFTED TO SERVE

REFLECTIONS FROM SESSION 2

1. If you committed Philippians 2:1–5 to memory, would you be willing to say this passage for your group? What have you learned about God's plan for your life through this passage?
2. If you took time to communicate thanks to a person who has been an example of servanthood to you, how did that person respond?

THE BIG PICTURE

The old adage says hindsight is 20/20. The truth is, sometimes we understand things better long after the fact. As I look back on my life, I realize that I didn't know anything about spiritual gifts for much of my life. Even though I grew up in a church my whole life, went to Christian grade schools, Christian high school, and Christian college, I still really didn't know a whole lot about spiritual gifts.

I learned about spiritual gifts by seeing them at work in real life. I started my teaching ministry in the mid-seventies with a group of twenty-five high school students. This group of young people had an unusual love for each other and started to develop an intense concern for their unchurched high school friends. Realizing this deep concern, we began planning a youth program that would reach those friends.

As we met to strategize, the ideas started to fly. What we put together in those brain-storming sessions was the pilot ministry for what eventually evolved into Willow Creek Community Church. We realized that this kind of an intensive, outward-focused ministry was going to take an enormous amount of work. We knew that no one or two people would be able to do it all; it was going to take a team effort.

I can remember one person saying, "Well, I can play a musical instrument." We all said, "That's good. You play your instrument." Someone else said, "I can sing a little bit." One high school student said, "I can't play an instrument or sing, but I could set up the music stands, chairs, and microphones. Is that of any value?" We all said, "Yeah, we need that!" Another one said, "I can take pictures and make a slide presentation with some music. Maybe that would be helpful."

One by one they continued to say how each one could contribute: "I'm sort of good at leading people. If we ever get large enough to break up the group into subgroups, I could lead one of those." "How about if we did a little drama? I think I could put some skits together." "I'm pretty artistic. I could make some banners we could hang on the walls when the kids come. Maybe that would help brighten the place up." "I could go to the different high schools and parks after school and talk to kids. I think I would be good at inviting people." I remember a 15-year-old who said he would like to do lighting. We didn't have the faintest idea of what he meant, but we all said, "Go for it!" And he did!

At the time, we had no idea we were beginning to establish a biblically functioning community based on spiritual gifts. We were just trying to offer whatever we had to God in service. It was only along the way that we discovered we were using spiritual gifts to serve God and others.

A WIDE ANGLE VIEW

1

What is one way you serve others that feels natural and brings you joy?

How can using this ability add to the lives of others?

A BIBLICAL PORTRAIT

Read 1 Corinthians 12:1, 7–11, 14–26

2 What various spiritual gifts are listed in this passage?

What do you notice about the diversity of these gifts? What are some of the different ways these gifts can be used?

3 The apostle Paul compares the church to a physical body. What are some of the ways the two are similar?

4 Respond to one of these statements:

Let's be honest, there are some people in the church who are just dead weight. We would be better off without them!

I have nothing to offer in the life of the church. If I left, no one would ever miss me.

SHARPENING THE FOCUS

Read Snapshot "Spiritual Gifts Defined"

SPIRITUAL GIFTS DEFINED

If we are going to dig into the topic of spiritual gifts, we need to have a clear and basic working definition so that we are all talking about the same thing. I would define spiritual gifts this way: *Spiritual gifts are divine enablements or special God-given abilities entrusted to every follower of Christ in order to involve them in the task of advancing His purposes.* Every believer has at least one spiritual gift. They are given by God, according to His plan and design.

With that kind of understanding you can see why spiritual gifts are so important: They are God's way of engineering a plan for all of His people to do work together, just like a body. All of us have vastly different backgrounds, personalities, upbringings, socioeconomic standings, and histories. Yet every member of the church matters to God, and they should matter to us. Only when all of us discover, develop, and use our gifts can the church be healthy and strong.

5

What is one spiritual gift God has given you and how are you using it to help advance His purposes?

If you are not sure what your spiritual gift is, what is one area of ministry or service that excites you and that you would like to know more about?

Read Snapshot "The Thrill and Joy of Using Your Gifts"

THE THRILL AND JOY OF USING YOUR GIFTS

I know countless people who have been smitten by a passion for service. They love to use their spiritual gifts for God's glory. They find joy in being used. They say, "It is a joy to serve, to count, to be a soldier, to make a contribution. This is what life is all about!"

There are so many people today wandering around without a purpose. Creatures existing without a cause. People who don't know what it is to count. So they just go through the motions of life, never connecting, never knowing what God designed them to be.

I would dare to say you haven't lived until you have felt the thrill of being used by God. In my lifetime I have flown and jumped out of airplanes, raced Corvettes and yachts, and done many other things people say bring thrills to life. Let me tell you, this is all kid stuff. You discover the major-league thrills in life when you identify your spiritual gift, experiment with it, use it, develop it, and feel God working through you. It is an amazing phenomenon. There is no greater thrill, no higher high, no more fulfilling experience in life. It is simply the best!

6 Describe a time that you had a clear and profound sense that God used you to bring Him honor or to touch the life of another person.

What makes this experience so memorable?

Read Snapshot "Receiving the Gifts"

RECEIVING THE GIFTS

The Holy Spirit distributes spiritual gifts. There is no need for any of us to say things like, "Well, I would like to have that gift" or "Boy, did God get His wires crossed when He gave me that gift." God knows you better than you know yourself. He knows what gift best suits who you are.

For years I tortured myself with feeling inadequate about teaching or preaching. I said, "I am not a polished communicator. I'm a mutt, a broken vessel." God just kept affirming me by His Spirit saying, "I have gifted you. Don't question Me. Just acknowledge My gift to you and run with it. Trust Me!" So I have tried to do the best I can with the gifts He gave me.

God has gifted you according to His wisdom. He took into consideration your personality, intelligence, natural talents, abilities, and future potential, and then He gifted you. Trust Him! He knows you inside and out. Every believer has at least one spiritual gift, and you are no exception.

7

What would you communicate to a person who says:

My gifts are used mostly behind the scenes, but I really wish I had the gift of teaching. I would love to get up in front of others and be in the spotlight.

I know I have the gift of leadership, but I get tired of the pressures being a leader can bring.

I wish I had a different gift that was more behind the scenes.

8

What is one area of giftedness you sense God is wanting you to investigate or develop?

How can your group members encourage you as you seek to grow in this area of giftedness?

PUTTING YOURSELF IN THE PICTURE

Use Your Gift

God expects us to use our gifts and holds us accountable for their development. God will not hold you accountable for the development of gifts He *didn't* give you. If you don't have the gift of mercy, God doesn't expect you to dive into all the compassion ministries of your church. However, He does expect us to develop the gifts we have. He wants leaders to lead, evangelists to communicate their faith, helpers to help, and intercessors to pray. Take time this week to make a list of the areas in which you are serving the Lord. Identify what spiritual gifts you are using in each ministry. Find at least one way you can develop and sharpen one of your gifts in the coming month.

Learning About Spiritual Gifts

Talk with your church leaders and discover if there is a class offered in your church where you can learn more about spiritual gifts. If there is, take this class and learn all you can. If there isn't, meet with your pastor and offer to help begin a class on this topic. If you don't have a resource to use for such a class, consider using the Network curriculum (for more details see Leader's Notes). Commit yourself to helping your church grow in its commitment to learn more about spiritual gifts.

THE SERVANT'S SURVIVAL KIT

REFLECTIONS FROM SESSION 3

1. If you committed yourself to grow in one area of gifted-ness, what is the area you chose and what are you doing to grow in this area of ministry?
2. If you investigated what kind of classes your church offers on discovering and developing spiritual gifts, tell your group what you learned. If your church does not have a class on this topic, what can you do as a group to help begin such a class?

THE BIG PICTURE

Most of us are familiar with what a bell-shaped curve is. Somewhere along the line in our education most of us have worked with bell-shaped curves. If you don't know what one is, here is a simple illustration:

Basic bell-shaped curve

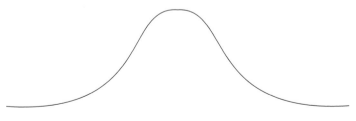

It looks like a flat line with the Liberty Bell in the middle. The reason the bell-shaped curve has become such a phenomenon in the study of statistics is that it represents the life cycle of certain kinds of products. For instance, if I were to give you an indication of the life cycle of the hula hoop, it would look like this:

Bell-shaped curve with figures for the hula hoop

Late 1950s and 1960s (Heavy sales and popularity)

Early 1950s   1970s

1930s and 1940s   1980s and 1990s
(No sales)   (Very limited sales)

When was the last time you purchased a hula hoop? The truth is, there just are not many sold these days. Maybe an occasional purchase for nostalgia's sake, but let's face it, the craze is over! The bell-shaped curve has hit a flat line!

How about CB radios? Do you remember them? There was a time nobody knew what a CB was but a few truckers. Then, the general public caught on and the sales went through the roof! The CB radio hit the top of that bell-shaped curve and people all over the place were saying, "10–4, Good Buddy!" However, by the mid-seventies the sales began to level off. By the end of the seventies, CBs were out of style. The craze was over and the old bell-shaped curve hit bottom again.

How many fads and products have experienced this same up-and-down trend? From mood rings to pet rocks to Power Rangers to "Tickle Me" Elmo, this pattern repeats itself over and over again! You can see why bell-shaped curves are a standard kind of picture on the graphs in many corporate headquarters across the country. These are the types of things that boards of directors have to really be concerned about when they are running companies.

Now, let's go into the board rooms of most churches. Let's look up on the wall and see if this life cycle exists in the pattern of Christian service. Let's look at the average path many Christians take once they meet Christ and discover their spiritual gifts. They tend to enter the arena of Christian service with excitement and passion. This man or woman has never really thought of serving and giving sacrificially, but now they are ready to serve with all their might. The curve of service begins to climb. They say "yes" to everything. They want to help, to serve, to give, to make a difference. However, with time, their enthusiasm and commitment plateau. They just can't give any more, their schedule is full, they start growing tired of all the things they "have to do!" They have good reasons, but the level of their Christian service is starting to dip noticeably. Over time they finally bail out. "Let someone else do it! I've served my time," is their battle cry. The cycle has gone from beginning to end and the bell-shaped curve has hit bottom.

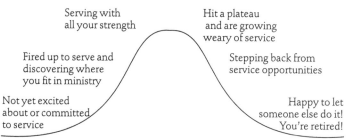

This is a sad picture, but all too often it is repeated in the lives of followers of Christ and in churches all over the world.

A WIDE ANGLE VIEW

1   Take a moment and plot your life cycle of service on the bell-shaped curve below. Where do you see yourself in this diagram right now?

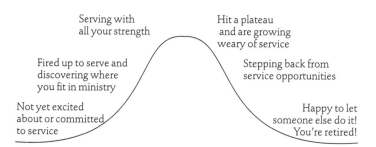

A BIBLICAL PORTRAIT

Read 1 Corinthians 15:58 and Galatians 6:9–10

2 Paint a verbal picture of what it looks like to do one of the following:

- "Always give yourselves *fully* to the work of the Lord."
- "Let us do good to *all* people, especially to those who belong to the family of believers."

3 In both of these passages, if we follow them to the letter, we realize that service has the potential to wear us out! What warning do you hear God giving through these words:

- "Stand firm. Let nothing move you."

- "Let us not become weary in doing good."

Have you experienced weariness in doing good? Or were you perhaps simply "busy"?

SHARPENING THE FOCUS

Read Snapshot "Faulty Motivation"

FAULTY MOTIVATION

The right motivation for Christian service is love. When we discover God loves us with an everlasting love and that we matter deeply to Him, we want to serve. He has given us salvation as a free gift. He has done for us what we could never do for ourselves. He has shed the blood of His most precious Son as a sin sacrifice for undeserving souls like ourselves. When all of that comes together and clicks, an unquenchable, divine energy is infused into the spirit of a believer. There is an insatiable desire to return love to God. That love is returned to God through worship and service. It is so natural that anything short of passionate service seems unnatural.

One major cause of servant drop-out is faulty motivation. Some people are motivated to serve because of guilt. They feel bad if they don't do something, so they say yes to soothe their own guilty conscience. Others are motivated by the belief that they must earn their way into God's favor and pave the way to heaven with their good works. There are also those who serve for the applause of people. They want others to notice their service and give them affirmation and praise. With the wrong kind of motivation, you won't be able to keep a servant serving. With the right kind of motivation, you won't be able to stop a servant from serving. It is just about that simple.

---

4 What will service look like when it is driven by one of these motivations:

- The need to soothe personal feelings of guilt
- A desire to earn God's good favor
- A need to be praised by others

Describe a time in your life of service that you were driven by one of these faulty motivations.

5 Bob is a follower of Christ and is serving with the false motivations listed in question four. Jane has been gripped by the amazing love of God and she is moved to serve as a response to God's love. Contrast these two servants in *one* of the following areas:

	Bob	Jane
Attitude when service is difficult	•	•
Feelings when no one says, "Thanks for your service."	•	•
Response when asked to serve for the "long haul"	•	•
Answer when asked to serve in an area no one will notice	•	•

Read Snapshot "Spiritual Gifts"

SPIRITUAL GIFTS

A second reason a servant's spirit sags is when they are serving outside their gift area. The previous session focused on the importance of serving in accordance with our spiritual gifts. Sadly, too many people serve outside their gift area. The Bible teaches that when you discover your spiritual gift (you might have more than one) and when you use it properly, you will tend to be charged up. On the other hand, when you are operating outside of your gift area, there will be depletion, frustration and exhaustion at almost every juncture.

6 Describe a time you have served in an area where you were not gifted. How did this impact your level of motivation?

Describe a time you served in a ministry that matched your spiritual gifts. How did this impact your motivation and energy level?

Read Snapshot "Too Much Service!"

TOO MUCH SERVICE!

A third cause for a sagging servant's spirit is too much service. Often a highly motivated believer doesn't think this is possible. They say, "I am going to burn out instead of rust out." Sadly, many of them do just that. They burn out. There is a great deal of misunderstanding about this kind of thing in the Christian community. A lot of Christians run around saying "More service is better service. Busyness is next to godliness. God loves those who live on the edge of exhaustion." They are out helping others seven nights a week and they wear their neck-breaking schedule like a badge of spirituality. But, with time, the load becomes too heavy and they crash. I have seen it and it is never a pretty sight. These faithful and frenzied servants just can't keep up this superhuman pace over the long haul.

7 What are some of the consequences when we overdose on service?

8 What does a healthy life of service look like?

If you are under-serving right now, how can your group members encourage you to serve more faithfully?

39

If you are over-serving, how can your group members keep you accountable to slow the pace and find balance in your life of service?

PUTTING YOURSELF IN THE PICTURE

Taking Time for Self-Care

Have you been neglecting self-care? Do you ever brag that you would rather burn out than rust out? Maybe you think you are going to be a hero and defy the realities of life. Maybe you think you can serve at a break-neck pace and never crash. Here is the hard truth . . . you can't. You will be a statistic. Your life of service will be a bell-shaped curve.

You may be serving in four or five areas and need to cut back to two or three areas. Don't risk burnout! Adjust these things before you blow out. God wants you to flourish and be thrilled with what you do in the body of Christ. This can only happen when you honestly evaluate your life and make sure you are not on the burnout fast track.

Take time in the coming week and reflect on the following questions:

How much time do you spend on a weekly basis in prayer, Bible study, and personal spiritual growth?

How much time do you spend on a weekly basis with your family members?

How much time do you spend on a weekly basis exercising, resting, and caring for your physical health?

How much time do you spend on a weekly basis in your vocation?

How much time do you spend on a weekly basis with friends and in recreational activities?

Where do you need to spend more time and energy?

Where do you need to spend less time and energy?

A Motivation Check

Take time in the coming week to do a service motivation check. Be brutally honest with yourself and God.

What motivates you to serve?

- _____
- _____
- _____
- _____
- _____
- _____

How should your motivation change in specific areas of Christian service? Who can pray for you and encourage you as you seek proper motivation in your life of service?

SERVING THROUGH SHARING

REFLECTIONS FROM SESSION 4

1. If you took time to evaluate your schedule and the role of service and self-care in your life, what did you discover? What is one change you will be making in your schedule and lifestyle?

2. If you took time to reflect on your motivation for service, what good motivations did you find? What is one motivation you feel prompted to change? Who is one person who will be praying for you as you seek to be changed in this area of motivation?

THE BIG PICTURE

Some years ago I was speaking at a small Christian college just outside of New York City. The college had been declining for a number of years. The enrollment and morale were at a low point. I spent three days speaking to the student body, meeting with the faculty and administration, and trying to encourage these brothers and sisters. On the final day, a few of the student leaders cornered me in the dining hall and asked me the big question, "Why doesn't anybody want to serve around here?"

There was an empty Styrofoam cup on my tray and the Holy Spirit prompted me to use it as an object lesson. I picked it up and acted as if I were trying to pour something out. Of course nothing came out—it was empty. Then I shook it a little bit and pounded on the bottom of the cup—still nothing! The students just stared at me as I made a number of efforts to shake something out of this empty cup.

Finally I said, "Empty glasses don't have much to pour out, do they?" I asked these discouraged but sincere leaders, "How can empty students be excited about servanthood?" You see, they were trying to shake something out of cups that were empty.

Empty people can't serve any more than empty cups can produce something to drink. But if you take a cup and fill it right up to the top, all you have to do is nudge it a little bit and its contents will spill over freely. When a person is filled with Christ, springs of living water will refuel, refresh, and refurbish parched lives. When the cup of a person's life is full, they serve out of surplus. They have something to give and it is a joy to spill over to others, to spend and be expended.

A WIDE ANGLE VIEW

1 What fills you up and makes you ready to serve?

What empties you out and makes it hard to serve?

If you were to describe your life like a Styrofoam cup, how full or empty are you today?

A BIBLICAL PORTRAIT

Read 2 Corinthians 12:14–15; 1 Thessalonians 2:6–9

2 In 2 Corinthians 12:15, Paul says, "I will very gladly spend for you *everything* I have." He even goes so far as to say that he will expend even himself. How did the apostle Paul spend himself in his service of the churches and people he loved?

3 When Paul describes his love and care for others in 1 Thessalonians 2:7, he uses the image of a mother caring for her children. With real life examples, describe how a mother serves and shares herself with her children.

How can this image of selfless servanthood shape our view of how we care for each other?

SHARPENING THE FOCUS

Read Snapshot "Sharing Ourselves"

SHARING OURSELVES

One way we serve other people is through sharing ourselves. In 1 Thessalonians 2:8 the apostle Paul says, "We loved you so much that we were delighted to share with you not only the gospel of God but *our lives as well.*" Paul was not content to simply tell these people the message of Christ, he wanted to invest his own life in their lives.

In the past sessions we have looked at God's call for us to serve by using our spiritual gifts. But, using our gifts is only part of the story. We need to learn how to share our lives with others. A secure, mature, joyful, spirit-filled servant doesn't fear the notion of getting personally involved and wrapped up in the lives of others; self-disclosure is part of the job description. Vulnerability, transparency, and a willingness to dive elbow deep into the lives of people is part of our call as servants. If we are not ready to invest our lives, we are not ready to be God's servants.

4 Describe someone who served you with his or her spiritual gift(s) and how he or she made an investment in your life.

How has that person's investment impacted you as a follower of Christ?

5

How can you invest yourself more fully in the life of someone in *one* of these areas:

- In your home with one of your children
- In your home with your spouse
- With someone in your neighborhood
- With a seeker with whom you have established a friendship
- With a person who is part of your church

Read Snapshot "Sharing Our Skills, Talents, and Abilities"

SHARING OUR SKILLS, TALENTS, AND ABILITIES

Another way we can expand the horizons of our servanthood is by sharing our skills and abilities with others. The Bible clearly communicates that in the family of believers we should not only share our gifts with one another, but we should also be enthusiastically and eagerly sharing our talents, learned skills, and abilities. Most church congregations are comprised of more highly skilled people than you can shake a stick at! There are those who can repair appliances, cars, and bicycles, those who are skilled in investment and money management techniques, those who have talents and abilities in the areas of painting, carpentry, plumbing, electronics, computers, dental and medical care, landscaping, education, cooking, management, estate planning, and the list just goes on and on and on. How pleased our Lord would be if all of us, with whatever learned skill or developed ability we have, would take those talents and use them in the service of others.

6

Describe a time you used a skill, talent, or ability to serve someone in one of these areas:

- In your neighborhood
- In another culture or country
- In your church

How did it feel when you used this ability to help another person?

7

What is one talent or skill you have that you want to offer God today?

Who will you serve with this ability and when will you serve them?

Read Snapshot "Sharing Our Material Resources"

SHARING OUR MATERIAL RESOURCES

One final way you can serve through sharing is by making your money and possessions available to others. This kind of sharing broke out without warning in the early church. (Read Acts 2:42–47 and 4:32–37. . . it's amazing!) People started selling their property and coming to the church with their gifts. They laid them at the apostles' feet so that the work of the Lord could flourish. This same Spirit-inspired generosity has occurred throughout history and still happens every day. People give small, medium, and large gifts, vehicles, equipment, and every imaginable material item needed to show God's love to others. When the love of God penetrates a heart, the idol of materialism falls and people become generous.

8

Is there a material need in your church right now that your group could meet together? How can you use your combined resources to serve *one* of these groups in your church?

- The church nursery
- The children's ministry
- The youth group
- Those who are shut-ins because of health or age
- Some other area of need

PUTTING YOURSELF IN THE PICTURE

PERSONAL SKILL AND TALENT ASSESSMENT

Take time to identify at least five distinct abilities you have that could be offered to others in service. Remember, you don't have to use all of them at once. Also, be mindful that every need you encounter does not mean you are called to meet this need. This exercise is simply an opportunity for you to begin identifying some areas where you might have an opportunity to serve and invest yourself in the lives of others some time in the future.

Skills, talents, and abilities I have in my service arsenal:

1. _____

2. _____

3. _____

4. _____

5. _____

GIVE IT AWAY!

There is great freedom when we learn to give things away. Identify one item you have that you could give to someone or some organization as an act of service. Pray for God to grow and stretch you through this experience.

My Life, a Living Sacrifice

Reflections from Session 5

1. If you took time to assess what skills, talents, and abilities you have in your service arsenal, what did you discover about yourself? How can you use this knowledge in service to God and others?
2. If you gave something away since your last meeting, tell about this experience and how it felt.

THE BIG PICTURE

The theme of sacrifice runs through the entire Bible like a crimson thread. All the way back in the book of Genesis Adam and Eve sinned and rebelled against God. We read that God covered the shame of their nakedness with animal skins. Think about that for a minute—God had to slay innocent animals in order to provide those skins to cover Adam and Eve. Imagine Adam and Eve's shock and horror as they witnessed death for the first time and then had the skins taken and put around them to cover their nakedness. Do you see the image? The innocent animal is slaughtered, and the guilty parties are covered.

In the book of Exodus, the element of sacrifice is brought to the front once again. The people of Israel are captives in the land of Egypt. God sends nine plagues on the land, but the king of Egypt will still not release the people. Finally, the tenth plague is announced to Moses. The angel of death is going to visit every home in all of the land, slaying the firstborn son in each home unless the blood of an innocent lamb is sprinkled on the doorpost of the house. If the angel sees the blood over the doorpost, he will pass over that house. The crimson blood of an innocent lamb is the only hope for the eldest boy of each household.

Still later, the Old Testament sacrificial system is put into place. God institutes all kinds of sacrifices, specifying the need for guilt offerings, drink offerings, burnt offerings, sin offerings, and many other sacrifices. Among the various sacrifices, God institutes the Day of Atonement, the day when all the people came together to confess their sins before a holy God. Then, an unblemished lamb was slaughtered in front of all of the people. Its blood soaked the ground, a visible sign of the transference of guilt from the people onto the innocent animal. The lamb was the substitute—the sin sacrifice—taking the punishment that should have been given out to the people.

In Isaiah 53 the crimson thread is seen again. The prophet announces that an innocent person, this time a human being, is going to be the ultimate sin sacrifice. Isaiah 53:5 says, "But he was pierced for our transgressions, he was crushed for our iniquities; the punishment that brought us peace was upon him, and by his wounds we are healed." The people began to understand that someday there would be a final sin sacrifice, once and for all, to bear the punishment they deserved. Isaiah was pointing to Jesus.

In the New Testament, John the Baptist speaks concerning Jesus, "Behold, the Lamb of God who takes away the sins of the world." John used sacrificial language so that all the people would understand that Jesus was the sacrifice promised by Isaiah centuries before. Jesus would be the final sacrificial Lamb of God, slaughtered so that His shed blood could pay for the sins of the world.

Do you ever wonder what it would have been like to stand at the foot of the cross and watch the innocent Lamb of God spill His blood for your sins so that we could go free? At the end of Jesus' torturous dying, while hanging on the cross, He shouted, "It is finished!" The final sacrifice had been made.

A WIDE ANGLE VIEW

1 What is one of the greatest sacrifices another person has made for you?

How has that person's sacrifice influenced your relationship with him or her?

A BIBLICAL PORTRAIT

Read Hebrews 13:11–16

2 How does this passage portray the following sacrifices:

- Animal sacrifices of the Old Testament

- The sacrifice of Jesus

- The sacrifice we should offer to God

3 What are the results of the sacrifice of Jesus?

What are the results of our sacrifice to God?

SHARPENING THE FOCUS

Read Snapshot "The Sacrifice of Our Lips"

THE SACRIFICE OF OUR LIPS

One of the ways we offer our lives as a living sacrifice to God is by lifting up praise with our lips. God's heart fills with joy when He hears expressions of worship from His children. When we pour out from our hearts to God, He basks in the warmth of our praise. When we realize what He has done for us and open our lips in praise and worship . . . this is a sacrifice that is pleasing to God. Learn to praise God with your words. Do it honestly. Do it often. Stretch yourself. Challenge yourself. Do it privately. Do it corporately. But let His praise always be on your lips.

---

4 What is one thing you want to praise God for today?

5 What is one of God's character traits that causes you to worship Him?

Read Snapshot "The Sacrifice of Our Hands"

THE SACRIFICE OF OUR HANDS

Another aspect of offering our lives as a living sacrifice is committing ourselves to doing good and sharing with others. God loves to see us pour out our lives for one another. He rejoices when husbands pour out their lives to their wives and wives to their husbands. Our Maker celebrates when parents sacrificially pour out their lives for their children and children for their parents. Our Father is delighted when we seek to serve our friends. The heart of Jesus is warmed when His followers do good to those who are seeking after God.

How should you respond to Christ's sin sacrifice? Pour out your heart to people like an offering. Give yourself away. God says, "I love that. I accept servanthood as an acceptable sacrifice of praise."

---

6 What is an act of sacrifice and service you could offer to *one* of these people:

- A friend
- A seeker
- A family member
- A church member
- A neighbor
- A coworker

How can your group members pray for you and encourage you in this commitment?

Read Snapshot "The Sacrifice of Our Resources"

THE SACRIFICE OF OUR RESOURCES

In Philippians 4:18 the apostle Paul says that money given to the Lord's work is an acceptable sacrifice. The terminology he uses is of a fragrant aroma, a sweet-smelling sacrifice pleasing to God: "I have received full payment and even more; I am amply supplied, now that I have received from Epaphroditus the gifts you sent. They are a fragrant offering, an acceptable sacrifice, pleasing to God."

Paul had received a monetary gift from the Christians in Philippi, but he saw it as a sacrifice to God! In the same way, when we give generously, this is a pleasing sacrifice to God.

7 How have you experienced giving as an act of sacrifice and worship?

How could you deepen your worship of God by giving more sacrificially?

8 How has your understanding of yourself as a servant been shaped and impacted over these six sessions on servanthood?

What is one new way you are serving God and others because of this study?

PUTTING YOURSELF IN THE PICTURE

MAKING A SACRIFICE

In this session you focused on three practical ways to make your life a living sacrifice. Reflect on one way you can deepen your sacrificial service in each of the following areas:

- How can you deepen your worship of God with your lips?
- What act of service can you do for someone in need?
- What is one material gift you can give to God or to a person in need?

Pray for God to give you a deep sense of worship and joy as you learn to offer your life as a living sacrifice to Him. Offer Him praise by writing out a personal psalm of adoration to Him. Using Psalm 146 as an example, give God your own words and thoughts.

MY OFFERING

Pray for God to make your whole life a living sacrifice to Him. Take time in the coming week to memorize Romans 12:1–2 and reflect on what it means to give yourself fully to God.

Therefore, I urge you, brothers, in view of God's mercy, to offer your bodies as living sacrifices, holy and pleasing to God—this is your spiritual act of worship. Do not conform any longer to the pattern of this world, but be transformed by the renewing of your mind. Then you will be able to test and approve what God's will is—his good, pleasing and perfect will.

LEADER'S NOTES

Leading a Bible discussion—especially for the first time—can make you feel both nervous and excited. If you are nervous, realize that you are in good company. Many biblical leaders, such as Moses, Joshua, and the apostle Paul, felt nervous and inadequate to lead others (see, for example, 1 Cor. 2:3). Yet God's grace was sufficient for them, just as it will be for you.

Some excitement is also natural. Your leadership is a gift to the others in the group. Keep in mind, however, that other group members also share responsibility for the group. Your role is simply to stimulate discussion by asking questions and encouraging people to respond. The suggestions listed below can help you to be an effective leader.

PREPARING TO LEAD

1. Ask God to help you understand and apply the passage to your own life. Unless that happens, you will not be prepared to lead others.
2. Carefully work through each question in the study guide. Meditate and reflect on the passage as you formulate your answers.
3. Familiarize yourself with the Leader's Notes for each session. These will help you understand the purpose of the session and will provide valuable information about the questions in the session. The Leader's Notes are not intended to be read to the group. These notes are primarily for your use as a group leader and for your preparation. However, when you find a section that relates well to your group, you may want to read a brief portion or encourage them to read this section at another time.
4. Pray for the various members of the group. Ask God to use these sessions to make you better disciples of Jesus Christ.
5. Before the first session, make sure each person has a study guide. Encourage them to prepare beforehand for each session.

LEADING THE SESSION

1. Begin the session on time. If people realize that the session begins on schedule, they will work harder to arrive on time.
2. At the beginning of your first time together, explain that these sessions are designed to be discussions, not lectures. Encourage everyone to participate, but realize some may be hesitant to speak during the first few sessions.
3. Don't be afraid of silence. People in the group may need time to think before responding.
4. Avoid answering your own questions. If necessary, rephrase a question until it is clearly understood. Even an eager group will quickly become passive and silent if they think the leader will do most of the talking.
5. Encourage more than one answer to each question. Ask, "What do the rest of you think?" or "Anyone else?" until several people have had a chance to respond.
6. Try to be affirming whenever possible. Let people know you appreciate their insights into the passage.
7. Never reject an answer. If it is clearly wrong, ask, "Which verse led you to that conclusion?" Or let the group handle the problem by asking them what they think about the question.
8. Avoid going off on tangents. If people wander off course, gently bring them back to the passage being considered.
9. Conclude your time together with conversational prayer. Ask God to help you apply those things that you learned in the session.
10. End on time. This will be easier if you control the pace of the discussion by not spending too much time on some questions or too little on others.

We encourage all small group leaders to use *Leading Life-Changing Small Groups* (Zondervan) by Bill Donahue and the Willow Creek Small Group Team while leading their group. Developed and used by Willow Creek Community Church, this guide is an excellent resource for training and equipping followers of Christ to effectively lead small groups. It includes valuable information on how to utilize fun and creative relationship-building exercises for your group; how to plan your meeting; how to share the leadership load by identifying, developing, and working with an "apprentice leader;" and how to find creative ways to do group prayer. In addition, the book includes material and tips on handling potential conflicts and difficult personalities, forming group covenants, inviting new members, improving listening skills, studying the Bible, and much more. Using *Leading Life-Changing Small Groups* will help you create a group that members love to be a part of.

Now let's discuss the different elements of this small group study guide and how to use them for the session portion of your group meeting.

The Big Picture

Each session will begin with a short story or overview of the lesson theme. This is called "The Big Picture" because it introduces the central theme of the session. You will need to read this section as a group or have group members read it on their own before discussion begins. Here are three ways you can approach this section of the small group session:

- As the group leader, read this section out loud for the whole group and then move into the questions in the next section, "A Wide Angle View." (You might read the first week, but then use the other two options below to encourage group involvement.)
- Ask a group member to volunteer to read this section for the group. This allows another group member to participate. It is best to ask someone in advance to give them time to read over the section before reading it to the group. It is also good to ask someone to volunteer, and not to assign this task. Some people do not feel comfortable reading in front of a group. After a group member has read this section out loud, move into the discussion questions.
- Allow time at the beginning of the session for each person to read this section silently. If you do this, be sure to allow enough time for everyone to finish reading so they can think about what they've read and be ready for meaningful discussion.

A Wide Angle View

This section includes one or more questions that move the group into a general discussion of the session topic. These questions are designed to help group members begin discussing the topic in an open and honest manner. Once the topic of the lesson has been established, move on to the Bible passage for the session.

A Biblical Portrait

This portion of the session includes a Scripture reading and one or more questions that help group members see how the theme of the session is rooted and based in biblical teaching. The Scripture reading can be handled just like "The Big Picture" section: You can read it for the group, have a group member read it, or allow time for silent reading. Make sure everyone has a Bible or that you have Bibles available for those who need them. Once you have read the passage, ask the question(s) in this section so that group members can dig into the truth of the Bible.

SHARPENING THE FOCUS

The majority of the discussion questions for the session are in this section. These questions are practical and help group members apply biblical teaching to their daily lives.

SNAPSHOTS

The "Snapshots" in each session help prepare group members for discussion. These anecdotes give additional insight to the topic being discussed. Each "Snapshot" should be read at a designated point in the session. This is clearly marked in the session as well as in the leader's notes. Again, follow the same format as you do with "The Big Picture" section and the "Biblical Portrait" section: Either you read the anecdote, have a group member volunteer to read, or provide time for silent reading. However you approach this section, you will find these anecdotes very helpful in triggering lively dialogue and moving discussion in a meaningful direction.

PUTTING YOURSELF IN THE PICTURE

Here's where you roll up your sleeves and put the truth into action. This portion is very practical and action-oriented. At the end of each session there will be suggestions for one or two ways group members can put what they've just learned into practice. Review the action goals at the end of each session and challenge group members to work on one or more of them in the coming week.

You will find follow-up questions for the "Putting Yourself in the Picture" section at the beginning of the next week's session. Starting with the second week, there will be time set aside at the beginning of the session to look back and talk about how you have tried to apply God's Word in your life since your last time together.

PRAYER

You will want to open and close your small group with a time of prayer. Occasionally, there will be specific direction within a session for how you can do this. Most of the time, however, you will need to decide the best place to stop and pray. You may want to pray or have a group member volunteer to begin the lesson with a prayer. Or you might want to read "The Big Picture" and discuss the "Wide Angle View" questions before opening in prayer. In some cases, it might be best to open in prayer after you have read the Bible passage. You need to decide where you feel an opening prayer best fits for your group.

When opening in prayer, think in terms of the session theme and pray for group members (including yourself) to be responsive to the truth of Scripture and the working of the Holy Spirit. If you have seekers in your group (people investigating Christianity but not yet believers) be sensitive to your expectations for group prayer. Seekers may not yet be ready to take part in group prayer.

Be sure to close your group with a time of prayer as well. One option is for you to pray for the entire group. Or you might allow time for group members to offer audible prayers that others can agree with in their hearts. Another approach would be to allow a time of silence for one-on-one prayers with God and then to close this time with a simple "Amen."

EXPOSING THE "ME-FIRST" MIND-SET

MARK 8:31—38

INTRODUCTION

In this first session of our study on Serving Lessons, I want to show you how Jesus took upon Himself the onerous and unpleasant task of exposing the seriousness of the "me-first" mind-set in the lives of His disciples. What I hope you will come to understand through this session and the following sessions is how difficult it is to loosen the grip of self-centeredness on any human being's life. "Me-first" mind-sets don't change easily—that is why they are called "mind-sets." Our view of ourselves and the world around us is developed over a long period of time. It is a way of looking at life, at relationships, at Christianity, at work, at kids, at church. It invades and influences all we think, say, and do.

As a leader, begin praying for yourself and each member of your group. The six sessions in this guide will dig into the heart of the human condition. They will uncover things we don't like to admit exist in ourselves or those we are close to. But if we can get through the discomfort of facing our own self-centeredness, we can discover the joy and freedom of a life filled with service to God and others.

THE BIG PICTURE

Take time to read this introduction with the group. There are suggestions for how this can be done in the beginning of the leader's section.

A WIDE ANGLE VIEW

Question One Two thousand years ago Jesus was exposing the lie of the "me-first" mind-set. He was saying, "Peter, and all the rest of you. Don't buy it. Every culture that comes down the pike will try to sell you the 'me-first' lie, because the culture is being influenced by Satan." Just as Jesus warned His first followers, His warnings are needed today. Every generation needs to have the "me-first" mind-set exposed for what it is . . . a lie, a delusion, a trap!

I didn't even know I had become a victim of the "me-first" culture during my teenage years. I was first confronted with a revolutionary look at life in college, under the teaching of one of my professors, Dr. Bilezikian. He stood in front of a class filled with "me-first" college students and said, "Students, true fulfillment will never come through self-gratification." That contradicted everything I was hearing in life. It contradicted everything I was feeling. Yet I could see that it came right out of Scripture, and it rang true in my spirit. Dr. B. would say, "Do you want to really live, students? True fulfillment comes only through faithful service to God and humble service to people." He would plead with us, "Give yourself to God and to service to others . . . then trust God for the rest. See what happens!"

I invite you to do the same. Commit yourself to a life of service and find joy beyond description.

A Biblical Portrait

Read Mark 8:31–38

Question Two You might think that Jesus could simply say, "No more of this 'me-first' mentality; it is time to have a 'Father-first' mind-set." But Jesus knew it would take more than this to make a dent in the steel-plated claws of self-centeredness. So He broached the subject by announcing to His disciples that He was going to lay down His life in an act of selfless servanthood. Jesus taught His followers that He, the Son of Man, would suffer many things. He would be rejected by the elders, the chief priests, and the scribes, and after being killed, He would rise again in three days. He was stating the matter plainly; there was no secret agenda here. He was the Lamb of God who was going to be slaughtered as the payment for sin.

But it is essential to remember that the disciples (Peter included) had already been under Jesus' ministry for over two years. They had witnessed many miracles, heard powerful preaching, and developed a great appreciation for the depth of His wisdom. We read that Peter took Jesus aside and rebuked Him. This action took a certain amount of courage. Try to imagine rebuking the Son of God! Still, I think Peter wanted Jesus to know that His death would be a pathetic waste of gifts, wisdom, and power.

I sometimes wonder if Peter's rebuke stemmed from a "me-first" reflex reaction to Jesus' plans to go to the cross. Remember, before Peter stumbled across the path of Jesus, he was a two-bit fisherman with a fairly predictable future. He had been a fisherman all of his life, and he was planning to be a fisherman for the rest of his life. Every day, he would go down to the seashore, take his boat out on the water, drop the nets, bring them up, count the fish, take them to the market, get his pay, buy some food, go home, sleep, and then get up the next morning to do it all over again.

Then he met Jesus. Ever since that day, things had been different. Peter had become the right-hand man of the most powerful, gifted, charismatic, and revolutionary leader of the day. Jesus was doing miracles, feeding and healing people, and raising the dead. Who knew where all of this was headed? Maybe Jesus would establish a new order or perhaps an earthly kingdom. Maybe He would even overthrow the Roman government. Peter dreamed that the sky was the limit. He was fixed to a star and his star was rising.

Question Three This "me-first" mind-set is *not* merely a psychological maladjustment. It is *not* something about which we can go to our neighborhood counseling center and say, "Could you help me work out this little psychological problem? I tend to be self-centered now and then." When Jesus says, "Get behind me, Satan," He is saying, "Peter, you have been sucked into a mind-set that has been scripted in hell. You are expressing an attitude that has been authored by Satan himself. If you hold that mind-set, it will cost you your fulfillment in life and your soul in eternity." I think Jesus is trying to rattle Peter's cage and say, "You have no idea the grip that Satan has on your mind. He has you believing you are the most important person in the world, and you're not."

SHARPENING THE FOCUS

Read Snapshot "Grappling with Greatness" before Question 4

Question Four Can you believe it? After Jesus' first full sermon on servanthood His followers were arguing about who was the greatest. Who was the most likely to replace Jesus? Who was the most gifted? In many ways the disciples were just like us: wanting to love Jesus and follow Him, but struggling with their own needs and desires to be the greatest.

All of us have signs that begin to surface when we are being controlled by a "me-first" mind-set. Take time as a group to share honestly about the symptoms you see in your life when this mind-set is taking over.

Read Snapshot "Indiscriminate Service" before Question 5

Question Five If we approach acts of service with a "me-first" mind-set, we may end up serving, but our service will be very limited. We will end up doing those things that have some payoff. We will serve only those who are in a position to repay our kindness. Instead, Jesus calls us to serve in a way that has no concern for what we gain in the process.

Question Six Take time as a group to think of some of the people Jesus served. His example should broaden our horizons of service. Jesus was glad to serve anyone who had a need—children and adults, men and women, religious leaders and prostitutes, the wealthy and the poor, tax collectors and fishermen, the religious and the demon-possessed.

Read Snapshot "I Want to Be First" before Question 7

Questions Seven & Eight All of us struggle with the seduction of living a "me-first" mind-set. If we are going to expose this way of thinking, we need to be specific about how it is creeping up in our lives. At the conclusion of this first session, invite group members to be specific about where they struggle with this "me-first" mind-set.

PUTTING YOURSELF IN THE PICTURE

Tell group members that you will be providing time at the beginning of the next meeting for them to discuss how they have put their faith into action. Let them tell their stories; however, don't limit their interaction to the two options provided. They may have put themselves into the picture in some other way as a result of your study. Allow for honest and open communication.

Also, be clear that there will not be any kind of a "test" or forced reporting. All you are going to do is allow time for people to volunteer to talk about how they have applied what they learned in your last study. Some group members will feel pressured if they think you are going to make everyone provide a "report." You don't want anyone to skip the next group because they are afraid of having to say they did not follow up on what they learned from the prior session. The key is to provide a place for honest communication without creating pressure and fear of being embarrassed.

Every session from this point on will open with a look back at the "Putting Yourself in the Picture" section of the previous session.

BREAKING THE BACK OF SELF-CENTEREDNESS

LUKE 19:1–10

INTRODUCTION

True servanthood is an essential ingredient in all of society's major institutions. At work, at home, or in the church, true servanthood is the only path to ultimate fulfillment in life. We need to cooperate with the Holy Spirit as He seeks to break the back of self-centeredness. Real fulfillment will only come when our "me-first" mind-set is replaced with a "Father-first" mind-set that moves us to service of God and others. This session focuses on three blows we can deal to the back of self-centeredness.

THE BIG PICTURE

Take time to read this introduction with the group. There are suggestions for how this can be done in the beginning of the leader's section.

A WIDE ANGLE VIEW

Question One In our culture we don't often have servants waiting on us hand and foot. We certainly don't have domestic servants who wash the feet of guests who might enter our home. However, there are many simple and common tasks we might decide we are above doing. You know the husband who believes doing the laundry is his wife's job or the wife who believes the yard work is the husband's job; the business person who always expects the secretary to bring him coffee; the pastor who hears one of the church toilets has overflowed and does not even consider going to help clean up. You get the picture.

Take time as a group to discuss some of the tasks we can feel we are above or prefer others would tend to.

A BIBLICAL PORTRAIT

Read Luke 19:1–10

Question Two This is a story about a chief tax gatherer whose name was Zacchaeus. A chief tax collector, for those who don't know much about first-century culture, was a master of extortion. He would use intimidation as he overcharged people for their taxes so he could stuff his own pockets full of their money. He would defraud people right and left, telling them they owed the Roman government more than they actually did and putting the difference in his own bank account. Everyone hated tax collectors, yet they all knew there was not a thing they could do about these practices.

Zacchaeus was just such a "me-first," self-centered man. He was rich, cunning, cold, callous, conniving, and cruel. The kind of guy that never changes but just gets worse and wealthier as the years go on.

If you are familiar with the story of Zacchaeus, however, you know that a miraculous metamorphosis occurred. As Jesus traveled through Jericho, He asked Zacchaeus if He could come to his house for dinner . . . and Zacchaeus was never the same. This old, hardened tax collector met Jesus face-to-face, received Him as the forgiver of his sins, and began life as a follower of Christ. Something dramatic happened to the heart of this self-centered man. This greedy, callous, self-centered, "me-first" maniac started sharing freely with the poor and began making four-fold restitution of former wrongs.

Question Three Jesus initiated the contact with Zacchaeus. He extended a hand and asked for a face-to-face meeting. This is always the case. God reaches out to lost people. At the same time, Zacchaeus was receptive. He invited Jesus first into his home as a guest and then into his life as Lord. Jesus let Zacchaeus know that he now had the treasures of heaven in his bank account, and Zacchaeus began serving others with his earthly treasures. Right in front of our eyes we see the back of self-centeredness broken by the love and forgiveness of Jesus.

SHARPENING THE FOCUS

Read Snapshot "Meeting Jesus" before Question 4

Question Four When I was sixteen years old I met Jesus face-to-face for the first time. I can still visualize exactly where I was at a summer camp in Wisconsin. I could take you right to the spot on the hill where I was walking back to my cabin. God brought Titus 3:5 to my mind, "He saved us, not because of righteous things we had done, but because of his mercy. He saved us through the washing of rebirth and renewal by the Holy Spirit." Up to this point I had been in church, I had learned the Bible stories, I had even tried to live as a servant. But I had still not really met Jesus face-to-face.

At that moment it dawned on me that I didn't have to spend the rest of my life scraping and clawing and trying to earn God's approval. I remember my mind just spinning as I kept thinking to myself, *I owe Him my life. I am never going to be the same. I owe Him everything. I want to give everything.* I can remember quietly saying, "Take my life and let it be, from this point on, committed completely to You!"

Take time as a group to share your first memories of meeting Jesus face-to-face. Even if you were raised in the church, as I was, there will be moments when your faith began to be real and personal. Share these moments of spiritual awakening.

Read Snapshot "Renewing Our Minds" before Question 5

Questions Five & Six I have learned over the years that servanthood is almost always the right answer. When I see the bumper sticker "The one who dies with the most toys wins," my heart is saddened. When I am in an airport and I go past a magazine rack that has a copy of *Self* magazine, I try to train my mind to say, "That's a dead-end road. If I adopt that mind-set and go down that path I will shipwreck everything. The 'me-first' road will be the end of my ministry, the end of my marriage, the end of my family. I can't afford that." The costs are high, and we have all seen examples of people who have paid prices beyond description.

Read Snapshot "Examples of Servanthood" before Question 7

Question Seven Do you know what will happen if you allow the Holy Spirit to renew your mind so that your reflex reaction is service to God and people? You will begin to experience life in all its fullness. When you serve people at work, it will begin to create all kinds of opportunities for discussions about Christ. When you begin a reflex-kind of servanthood at home, you will be rewarded with a gracious, healthy attitude in your marriage. When everyone in a congregation is serving, an infectious attitude pervades the church. What a way to live! The back of self-centeredness is broken by salvation through God's grace and then by the renewing of your mind.

We all have examples of people who live with a passionate commitment to service. This service comes naturally, because they have been captured by the love of God. These people inspire us to be more faithful in service to God and others. Celebrate those people God has used in your life to challenge you in your life of service.

PUTTING YOURSELF IN THE PICTURE

Challenge group members to take time in the coming week to use part or all of this application section as an opportunity for continued growth.

GIFTED TO SERVE

1 CORINTHIANS 12:1, 7—11, 14—26

INTRODUCTION

A critical aspect of service in the church is spiritual gifts. This session scratches only the surface of this topic. However, it is essential for all of your group members to understand the centrality of spiritual gifts for a biblically functioning community.

You might find that some of your group members have a deep and developed understanding of spiritual gifts. You might also have some group members who know very little about them. In either case, this session will encourage personal reflection on each person's giftedness and sense of God's leading in their life of ministry. If you see a need for more study on this topic as a group, you may want to follow up this study by going through the *Network* training curriculum on spiritual gifts. There are more details on this learning tool in the back of this study guide.

THE BIG PICTURE

Take time to read this introduction with the group. There are suggestions for how this can be done in the beginning of the leader's section.

A WIDE ANGLE VIEW

Question One In the early days of our youth ministry, we did not use the term *spiritual gift;* we simply helped people find the place in ministry that fit their passions, personality, and abilities. With time, it became clear that many of these people were doing the very thing God made them to do. Invite group members to express areas of service that just feel right to them and seem to fit naturally.

A BIBLICAL PORTRAIT

Read 1 Corinthians 12:1, 7–11, 14–26

Question Two The apostle Paul teaches that there are varieties of gifts, but the same Holy Spirit. In other words, there are a variety of ways that spiritual gifts can be expressed, but the same Lord is leading each person to use their gifts. Spiritual gifts are for the good of the community of faith, the church.

God wants each church to be a blessed, flourishing, vital, enriching body of believers, so He gifted every single believer in some way that they will be a blessing to the rest of the body. If we don't identify, develop, and use our spiritual gifts, we rob the fellowship of something it needs. If you don't use your spiritual gifts, you are actually *hurting* the church. This is serious business!

Question Three Take time as a group to really think about the many parallels between a physical body and the church (the body of Christ). The apostle Paul uses this comparison by the leading of the Holy Spirit for very good reasons. Push the imagery and comparison as far as you can and see what you learn. You might begin by asking, What can we say about the human body? Then ask, How is this true of the church?

Question Four In this passage the apostle Paul talks about some parts of the human body saying, "I don't belong" or "You don't belong." This kind of thinking seems absurd when talking about a hand, foot, eye, or ear. However, too often we feel people are dispensable. We look at others in the church and really believe we could do without them and what they offer to the body. We can even look at ourselves and feel we are not needed or important. Take time as a group to grapple with the implications of this perspective.

SHARPENING THE FOCUS

Read Snapshot "Spiritual Gifts Defined" before Question 5

Question Five I remember driving onto our church campus one morning in a torrential downpour. I was amazed to see some of the people on our grounds crew out in the rain working on making our road accessible for worshipers to come to the services. I talked to some of them after they finished paving. They were drenched head to toe, but they said, "You know, it felt good. We counted. We served. Thousands of people will drive on this road and be served by what we have done." They were using their gifts to serve God and others.

As you discuss this question, the answers don't have to be deep and profound. Small tasks of service are just as pleasing to God and inspiring to others. Open the door for a free exchange of stories about serving.

Read Snapshot "The Thrill and Joy of Using Your Gifts" before Question 6

Question Six I am thankful that there have been many times in which I have sensed God using me to make a difference in the lives of others through the use of my spiritual gifts. I can still remember one night about two-and-a-half years into our high school ministry back in the seventies. We had 700–800 kids coming to Son City. The Holy Spirit led me to give a message to challenge students to receive Christ. I worked and worked on that message, but it just wasn't coming together. I took walks around the block at midnight. I got up and went into the dining room at three o'clock in the morning and prayed. I was in agony that whole week. I remember several times that week thinking that if this is what it took to be a teacher, the price was too high.

I never did feel completely comfortable with what I prepared, but I decided to just get up in front of those students and give it my best shot. At the end I said, "Now how many of you, after hearing what it means to be a Christian, would like to receive Christ? How many of you want to repent of your sins and receive Christ as your Savior right here, right now, in front of your friends?" In the next few moments about 250 students stood up and expressed their desire to become followers of Christ. I can remember staying there until almost midnight, all of us counseling students and praying with them. After they were all gone, I went out the back door of the church, leaned against a wall, and just burst out crying. I thought, *I love being used by God. There is nothing greater in all the world.*

Read Snapshot "Receiving the Gifts" before Question 7

Questions Seven & Eight It is easy to look at our gifts and wish we had some other God-given abilities. Too often the grass looks greener on the other side of the spiritual-gift fence. The key is to remember that God is a lot wiser than we are. We need to thank Him for the gifts He has given us and develop them for His glory. It is a waste of time to sit around wishing we had some different gift. God, the Giver, is wiser than we are. Let's trust Him and invest our lives developing and using our gifts for His glory.

PUTTING YOURSELF IN THE PICTURE

Challenge group members to take time in the coming week to use part or all of this application section as an opportunity for continued growth.

THE SERVANT'S SURVIVAL KIT

1 CORINTHIANS 15:58; GALATIANS 6:9–10

INTRODUCTION

Most of us live with a "me-first" mind-set until we meet Christ. When we become His followers, we suddenly realize that we are loved with an everlasting love. When we discover the depth of His love, our attitude toward life and others changes radically. Now we have a hunger for service. A motivated young believer who has really found a relationship with Christ sees many opportunities to serve and moves into ministry opportunities. However, all too often this enthusiasm peaks, wanes, and falls off with time. God's design is that we would enter into meaningful service that fits who God has made us to be. This service should continue for a lifetime, not only for a few months or years. If you are going fulfill the call to Christian service, we must identify how to serve long-term. This is the focus of this session.

THE BIG PICTURE

Take time to read this introduction with the group. There are suggestions for how this can be done in the beginning of the leader's section.

A WIDE ANGLE VIEW

Question One Have group members take a few minutes to reflect on the pattern of service in their own life. There is no right or wrong answer to this question . . . as long as the answer is sincere. Encourage group members to be as specific as possible. If they can identify a specific time, with dates, years, or their age at certain points in this process, this will help make it more concrete. Allow time for each person who desires to tell their story to express where they have been and where they are today.

It may also be helpful to note that this process can repeat itself. Some people have gone through this cycle more than once in their life as a follower of Christ.

A Biblical Portrait

Read 1 Corinthians 15:58 and Galatians 6:9–10

Question Two The apostle Paul is very clear that we are all called to acts of service. We are not to give only a small part of ourselves—the leftovers, the extra time and energy—we are called to give ourselves completely to God's work. We are to "do good to all people." What a challenge! The life of a Christ follower is a call to give ourselves fully in service. This biblical call works itself out in many different ways.

Invite group members to paint a picture of how they see this biblical exhortation lived out in daily life. Take the general invitation to service and look at what it can look like in modern-day terms.

Question Three There is a myth in the minds of many Christians that if they are doing good things, they will never burn out. Too many people discover that this is a false understanding only after they crash! Take time to look closely at these biblical warnings. It is deeply important for each person to understand that God warns them to beware of service burn-out. Often people say, "It is a wise person who learns from his mistakes." This is true. However, the wiser person learns from other people's mistakes! The apostle Paul gives us warnings that each of your group members needs to hear loud and clear.

After looking at these warnings, take time for group members to tell their own stories of how they have learned this lesson.

Sharpening the Focus

Read Snapshot "Faulty Motivation" before Question 4

Questions Four & Five Many people serve with the wrong motivation. Some people join a fellowship and decide that if they are going to belong, they had better pay their dues. They want to be a good citizen. They say, "You know, I guess I ought to do something, so if someone asks me, I'll say yes." Unfortunately, their view of service reflect a country club, dues-paying mentality.

Other people get into a "works" motivation. They don't understand the free gift of God, which is eternal life through Jesus Christ, so they say, "I am going to appease the wrath of

God and earn my way into His good standing by serving night and day." They sign up for everything under the sun. They have a merit-focused mentality that thinks their service is going to gain them something in the eyes of God.

There are also those who serve to impress the leadership. They serve for the applause of others. They like the strokes, so they knock themselves out. Sadly, it is more for ego than for anything else. Some serve out of guilt or even boredom. Some people don't have a whole lot going on at home and just want to be busy doing something.

None of these motivations will sustain a servant over the long haul. One of the reasons we see many bell-shaped curves of servanthood is because people get into Christian service with a faulty fuel supply, a faulty motivation for service. They are motivated for a time, but that motivation runs out.

Read Snapshot "Spiritual Gifts" before Question 6

Question Six Many believers get all revved up about serving the Lord. They feel loved by God, they get motivated with the right motivation, they want to get out and serve, so they get elbow deep in all kinds of service. But even though they are motivated properly, they find out they don't really enjoy that particular area of service. What they are doing isn't a challenge. They are frustrated and experience no fulfillment. *How can this be?* they think. *My motivation is right! My heart is pure!*

People often hit the flat line of the bell-shaped curve after a service experience like this. Some avoid any kind of service in the future because they never feel the freedom to transfer out of one area that was obviously not their gift area into another area where maybe they could have thrived and flourished.

We need to learn to take this whole area of spiritual gifts seriously. God knows you inside and out, and He loves you. He wants for you to enjoy Christian service. He wants you to flourish in it and to feel freedom to be fulfilled in service. This means discovering your area of giftedness and learning to develop your spiritual gift. As mentioned in the leader's notes for session three, *Network* is one helpful resource for this listed in the back of this study guide.

Read Snapshot "Too Much Service!" before Question 7

Questions Seven & Eight You can have the right motivation for service and be serving in your gift area and *still* burn out. This happens when people simply take on too much service.

We need to develop a healthy balance between service and self-care.

An athlete who wants to be effective over the long haul takes a great interest in conditioning. This is also true for followers of Christ. To be properly motivated in our gift areas over the long haul, we must pay very special attention to how we manage our lives. We must make sure we are not so busy *working for* God that we don't have time to spend *communing with* Him. Sometimes we need to pass up some service opportunities so we can develop the quality of our walk with Christ. We should also be very careful about the quality of our family and marriage relationships. We will be held accountable before the Lord for the quality of our marriage, parenting, family life, and Christian service in the church. We should examine every area of life and be sure we are living in a way that honors Christ.

PUTTING YOURSELF IN THE PICTURE

Challenge group members to take time in the coming week to use part or all of this application section as an opportunity for continued growth.

SERVING THROUGH SHARING

2 CORINTHIANS 12:14—15; 1 THESSALONIANS 2:6—9

INTRODUCTION

Some of your group members will come with full cups. They will be so in touch with God's love and so connected to Christ that they are already spilling over with service. Others will enter your group session bone-dry and empty. Acknowledge this up front and encourage them to be open to God's filling in their lives. No matter how full or empty they are, God wants to help each person discover how to be filled more and how to overflow with service.

This session offers practical ways to express servanthood to one another. It will broaden the parameters of servanthood beyond the use of spiritual gifts. The use of our God-given spiritual gifts is essential, but there are other ways we can serve. Pray for each group member to discover how they can faithfully serve others by sharing what God has given them.

THE BIG PICTURE

Take time to read this introduction with the group. There are suggestions for how this can be done in the beginning of the leader's section.

A WIDE ANGLE VIEW

Question One It is important to start this session with an honest assessment of where each person is in his or her life of service. Some may feel empty, and others are overflowing. Invite each group member to reflect on where they are today and on what fills them up and depletes them.

A BIBLICAL PORTRAIT

Read 2 Corinthians 12:14–15 and 1 Thessalonians 2:6–9

Question Two One of the most challenging verses dealing with servanthood that I know is penned by the apostle Paul in 2 Corinthians 12:15. Paul says he would gladly spend and be expended for the sake of the Corinthian Christians. To me that is an amazing admission on Paul's part. Most of us guard ourselves very carefully so that we don't get used or used up. Paul says, "I love being expended in service toward you. I love being a servant, and I do so gladly." If you know anything about the church at Corinth, they weren't the easiest group to serve, but Paul was committed to pouring out his life for them.

The apostle Paul lived out his words in this passage. He poured himself out over and over again for the sake of the church and for those who were still seeking for God. You may want to take time to look at the following passages before your group meets. If you think it is appropriate, take time as a group and reflect on one or two of these passages: 2 Corinthians 6:3–10; 2 Corinthians 11:23–28; and Philippians 3:7–11.

Question Three The image of a loving and self-sacrificing mother is powerful. Take time as a group to unpack this image and let it sink in. This is the kind of heart and spirit of service God wants from all of us. After identifying some specific examples of motherly love, take time to identify principles and examples of how this image should shape our lives as servants.

SHARPENING THE FOCUS

Read Snapshot "Sharing Ourselves" before Question 4

Questions Four & Five There is a tremendous difference between a person who only shares his gift, and the person who imparts himself or herself as he shares his or her gift. Those who have the gift of teaching and who are willing to impart themselves to others don't just teach; they involve themselves with their learners and communicate much more than information or biblical data. They impart their own experience to the learners, their own failures and successes, their own victories and heartaches, their own emotion and energy. They pour out their soul. When this happens, the learners feel an outpouring of love and interest, and that makes a teacher much more than a teacher.

Servants who are willing to share their lives or impart themselves to others don't just visit afflicted people and say merci-
ful words to the brokenhearted. They crawl under the burden
in a personal way. As they are ministering to afflicted people,
they absorb some of the pain.

In John 11:35 we see Jesus weeping at the graveside of his
friend Lazarus. He was weeping because their lives had
become connected; they had poured out themselves to one
another. I think Jesus experienced deep hurt when Lazarus
died. Lazarus wasn't just a student to Jesus, he was a friend,
a brother.

We have all known people who poured out their lives as they
served us. Take time to tell the story of someone who served
you this way and how their life has impacted yours. Also discuss how you can grow as a servant who invests not only
your spiritual gifts, but also your own life.

Read Snapshot "Sharing Our Skills, Talents, and Abilities" before Question 6

Questions Six & Seven There are so many people in the
church who have needs that need to be met. There are also
those who have skills and abilities to meet these needs.
Imagine a church where needs are met and where church
members have the thrill of using their talents and abilities to
serve others. Some would experience the thrill of giving,
while others would experience the thrill of receiving. There
would be so much grace lubricating the fellowship that service would flow freely.

What a blessing we can be to other people when we take a
learned skill, a talent, and we say, "I want to serve you with
it." But a word of caution: Just because you have a learned
ability or skill and just because you see a need doesn't neces-
sarily mean that God wants you to meet it. You need the Holy
Spirit to give you guidance in each life situation. When you do
receive God's prompting to serve someone with your abilities, may I remind you of Jesus' words: "The Father who sees
in secret will richly reward you."

Read Snapshot "Sharing Our Material Resources" before Question 8

Question Eight Take time as a group to prayerfully identify
one way you can corporately use some material resources to
serve a group in your church. This kind of group service can
help clarify just how God can use you to serve and encourage
another follower of Christ or group of believers.

PUTTING YOURSELF IN THE PICTURE

Challenge group members to take time in the coming week to use part or all of this application section as an opportunity for continued growth.

MY LIFE, A LIVING SACRIFICE

HEBREWS 13:11—16

INTRODUCTION

The image of sacrifice is not one we are quick to discuss. The image of a dying animal is not attractive. The picture of Christ dying on the cross breaks our heart. The prospect of being poured out, personally, as a sacrifice is not appealing to many people. Let's admit it, sacrifice is not a popular topic.

At the same time, as followers of Christ, we have seen sacrifice weave its way through the entire Bible like a crimson thread. From the first sacrifice of an animal in the garden of Eden (to cover Adam and Eve's shame) to the Lamb of God slain before the foundation of the world in Revelation, sacrifice is at the core of our faith. We need to have our eyes opened to see the price God has paid for us and then to hear the call to offer our lives as a living sacrifice.

THE BIG PICTURE

Take time to read this introduction with the group. There are suggestions for how this can be done in the beginning of the leader's section.

A WIDE ANGLE VIEW

Question One We could all agree that Jesus has paid the ultimate sacrifice for us. The actions of any other person pale in comparison. It might be good, as a leader, to acknowledge this from the beginning of the session. This question is not designed to lead each person to say that Jesus has made the greatest sacrifice.

Invite group members to respond to the discussion question by telling about a person from their own life experience and how that person impacted their lives.

A Biblical Portrait

Read Hebrews 13:11–16

Question Two This passage touches on, and ties together, three kinds of sacrifice. First, it looks at the animal sacrifice of the Old Testament. Next, it looks at Jesus as the One who makes us holy through His shed blood. Finally, we are called to offer our sacrifice to God. Dig into the passage and discover the meaning of each of these sacrifices.

The clearest connection in this passage is the relationship of Jesus' sacrifice and the call for us to live lives of sacrifice to God. When you understand Jesus' sin sacrifice, a fire is ignited in the hearts of true believers that is fanned by the billows of the Holy Spirit.

Sometimes seekers think that dedication and service to Christ are a way of gaining God's approval or gaining entrance into the kingdom of heaven. That is not what our sacrifice is about. True devotion to Christ is motivated by Christ's sin sacrifice. We love Him and discover His love for us and we naturally crawl up on the altar and give ourselves to Him. We offer ourselves as living sacrifices in response to His sacrifice, which accomplished for us what we could never do for ourselves.

In the Old Testament God carefully instructed His people how to present acceptable sacrifices, offerings, and worship to Him. He described how His people could bring guilt offerings, drink offerings, burnt offerings, peace offerings, sin offerings, and many other sacrifices. God wanted those offerings brought to Him with a pure and willing spirit. He loved to see His people bring appropriate sacrifices of praise to Him. He still does. The goal for us is to discover what an appropriate sacrifice looks like today.

Question Three The book of Hebrews gives a window into what Jesus accomplished when He gave His life as a sacrifice for us. First, we are made holy. Through His shed blood, we are washed clean. This is a graphic and powerful picture, but if you see the crimson thread running through Scripture, it makes all the sense in the world.

> In fact, the law requires that nearly everything be cleansed with blood, and without the shedding of blood there is no forgiveness. (Heb. 9:22)

Jesus offers us purity and holiness through His shed blood. His sacrifice also opens the doors to heaven, "the city that is to come." Without the sacrificial death of Jesus, the way to eternity with the Father would still be closed.

When we offer our lives as living sacrifices, there are many results. The writer of Hebrews touches on a few of these. First, we will begin doing good to others. People matter to God, and when we offer our lives as sacrifices, we will begin serving others and doing good. This process involves sharing what we have with others. This sharing comes in the form of material good, spiritual truth, care, encouragement, or many other expressions of generosity. The final result is that God is pleased. Our lives poured out as a sacrifice to God bring joy to our Maker!

Sharpening the Focus

Read Snapshot "The Sacrifice of Our Lips" before Question 4

Questions Four & Five In Exodus 29 God outlines very carefully how certain sacrifices should be offered to Him. God is clear that specific situations require an offering that is placed on the altar early in the morning and is presented in such a way that the smoke and the aroma will rise heavenward *all throughout the day*. Then again in Exodus 29 He commands that another offering be given at twilight, another at dawn, and yet another at sunset. Why? The text says this should be done so there will be a continual aroma of worship going heavenward.

God does not ask us to praise and worship Him for twenty to thirty minutes each week at a worship service. He wants our lips praising Him all day long! He wants us exalting Him privately, communing with Him, lifting Him up, thinking of ways we can express adoration. Speak often of His goodness. Tell friends (believers and seekers) about the great things God has done. When we express our worship with our lips, an aroma comes from our lives that ascends to the throne of God.

Read Snapshot "The Sacrifice of Our Hands" before Question 6

Question Six The apostle Peter says in 1 Peter 2:5 that we are priests to one another. We all have the same Holy Spirit inside of us; therefore, we are to perform our priestly functions to each other as an acceptable sacrifice to God. We need to use our spiritual gifts as well as our talents and skills to do good for others. This is another way to offer our lives to God as a sacrifice that is pleasing to Him.

Every time a believer uses the gift of helps, God is registering that as a sacrifice of praise. Every time one of His followers writes a letter of encouragement, visits a sick person, teaches a Bible study, sings a musical number in church, takes part in a drama, uses administrative gifts, prays for the hurting, or ministers to another person, an acceptable offering is placed on the altar.

As you close this group of sessions on servanthood, encourage practical goals for actions of service. Invite group members to pray for each other and keep each other accountable to follow through on this goal.

Read Snapshot "The Sacrifice of Our Resources" before Question 7

Question Seven This question is intended to leave freedom to move in at least two directions. Some might respond by discussing how others have served them and what this has meant in their faith. Others may answer by telling about how they have grown through giving to others and offering sacrifices to God through their material resources.

Question Eight Allow time for celebration. Invite group members to communicate what God has been doing in their heart over the past six sessions. Rejoice in the way God is creating a desire and hunger to grow as servants.

PUTTING YOURSELF IN THE PICTURE

Challenge group members to take time in the coming week to use part or all of this application section as an opportunity for continued growth.

ADDITIONAL WILLOW CREEK RESOURCES

Small Group Resources

Coaching Life-Changing Small Group Leaders, by Bill Donahue and Greg Bowman
The Complete Book of Questions, by Garry Poole
The Connecting Church, by Randy Frazee
Leading Life-Changing Small Groups, by Bill Donahue and the Willow Creek Team
The Seven Deadly Sins of Small Group Ministry, by Bill Donahue and Russ Robinson
Walking the Small Group Tightrope, by Bill Donahue and Russ Robinson

Evangelism Resources

Becoming a Contagious Christian (book), by Bill Hybels and Mark Mittelberg
The Case for a Creator, by Lee Strobel
The Case for Christ, by Lee Strobel
The Case for Faith, by Lee Strobel
Seeker Small Groups, by Garry Poole
The Three Habits of Highly Contagious Christians, by Garry Poole

Spiritual Gifts and Ministry

Network Revised (training course), by Bruce Bugbee and Don Cousins
The Volunteer Revolution, by Bill Hybels
What You Do Best in the Body of Christ—Revised, by Bruce Bugbee

Marriage and Parenting

Fit to Be Tied, by Bill and Lynne Hybels
Surviving a Spiritual Mismatch in Marriage, by Lee and Leslie Strobel

Ministry Resources

An Hour on Sunday, by Nancy Beach
Building a Church of Small Groups, by Bill Donahue and Russ Robinson
The Heart of the Artist, by Rory Noland
Making Your Children's Ministry the Best Hour of Every Kid's Week, by Sue Miller and David Staal
Thriving as an Artist in the Church, by Rory Noland

Curriculum

An Ordinary Day with Jesus, by John Ortberg and Ruth Haley Barton
Becoming a Contagious Christian (kit), by Mark Mittelberg, Lee Strobel, and Bill Hybels
Good Sense Budget Course, by Dick Towner, John Tofilon, and the Willow Creek Team
If You Want to Walk on Water, You've Got to Get Out of the Boat, by John Ortberg with Stephen and Amanda Sorenson
The Life You've Always Wanted, by John Ortberg with Stephen and Amanda Sorenson
The Old Testament Challenge, by John Ortberg with Kevin and Sherry Harney, Mindy Caliguire, and Judson Poling

WILLOW
Willow Creek Association

Willow Creek Association
Vision, Training, Resources for Prevailing Churches

This resource was created to serve you and to help you build a local church that prevails. It is just one of many ministry tools that are part of the Willow Creek Resources® line, published by the Willow Creek Association together with Zondervan.

The Willow Creek Association (WCA) was created in 1992 to serve a rapidly growing number of churches from across the denominational spectrum that are committed to helping unchurched people become fully devoted followers of Christ. Membership in the WCA now numbers over 10,500 Member Churches worldwide from more than ninety denominations.

The Willow Creek Association links like-minded Christian leaders with each other and with strategic vision, training, and resources in order to help them build prevailing churches designed to reach their redemptive potential. Here are some of the ways the WCA does that.

- **A2: Building Prevailing Acts 2 Churches—Today**—an annual two-and-a-half day event, held at Willow Creek Community Church in South Barrington, Illinois, to explore strategies for building churches that reach out to seekers and build believers, and to discover new innovations and breakthroughs from Acts 2 churches around the country.

- **The Leadership Summit**—a once a year, two-and-a-half-day conference to envision and equip Christians with leadership gifts and responsibilities. Presented live at Willow Creek as well as via satellite broadcast to over one hundred locations across North America, this event is designed to increase the leadership effectiveness of pastors, ministry staff, volunteer church leaders, and Christians in the marketplace.

- **Ministry-Specific Conferences**—throughout each year the WCA hosts a variety of conferences and training events—both at Willow Creek's main campus and offsite, across the U.S., and around the world—targeting church leaders and volunteers in ministry-specific areas such as: evangelism, small groups, preaching and teaching, the arts, children, students, women, volunteers, stewardship, raising up resources, etc.

- **Willow Creek Resources®**—provides churches with trusted and field-tested ministry resources in such areas as leadership, evangelism, spiritual formation, spiritual gifts, small groups, stewardship, student ministry, children's ministry, the use of the arts-drama, media, contemporary music —and more.

- **WCA Member Benefits**—includes substantial discounts to WCA training events, a 20 percent discount on all Willow Creek Resources®, *Defining Moments* monthly audio journal for leaders, quarterly *Willow* magazine, access to a Members-Only section on WillowNet, monthly communications, and more. Member Churches also receive special discounts and premier services through WCA's growing number of ministry partners—Select Service Providers—and save an average of $500 annually depending on the level of engagement.

For specific information about WCA conferences, resources, membership, and other ministry services contact:

Willow Creek Association
P.O. Box 3188
Barrington, IL 60011-3188
Phone: 847-570-9812
Fax: 847-765-5046
www.willowcreek.com

Continue building your new community!
New Community Series
BILL HYBELS AND JOHN ORTBERG
with Kevin and Sherry Harney

Look for New Community at your local Christian bookstore.

Continue the Transformation
Pursuing Spiritual Transformation
JOHN ORTBERG, LAURIE PEDERSON,
AND JUDSON POLING

Look for Pursuing Spiritual Transformation at your local Christian bookstore.

TOUGH QUESTIONS

Garry Poole and Judson Poling

Softcover

How Does Anyone Know God Exists?	ISBN 0-310-24502-8
What Difference Does Jesus Make?	ISBN 0-310-24503-6
How Reliable Is the Bible?	ISBN 0-310-24504-4
How Could God Allow Suffering and Evil?	ISBN 0-310-24505-2
Don't All Religions Lead to God?	ISBN 0-310-24506-0
Do Science and the Bible Conflict?	ISBN 0-310-24507-9
Why Become a Christian?	ISBN 0-310-24508-7
Leader's Guide	ISBN 0-310-24509-5

REALITY CHECK SERIES

by Mark Ashton

Winning at Life	ISBN: 0-310-24525-7
Leadership Jesus Style	ISBN: 0-310-24526-5
When Tragedy Strikes	ISBN: 0-310-24524-9
Sudden Impact	ISBN: 0-310-24522-2
Jesus' Greatest Moments	ISBN: 0-310-24528-1
Hot Issues	ISBN: 0-310-24523-0
Future Shock	ISBN: 0-310-24527-3
Clear Evidence	ISBN: 0-310-24746-2

Network Revised

The Right People, in the Right Places, for the Right Reasons, at the Right Time

Bruce L. Bugbee and Don Cousins

Network Revised is a six-session dynamic program to help Christians understand who God has uniquely made them to be and to mobilize them to a place of meaningful service in the local church. Each participant in *Network Revised* will work through a series of assessments which leads them to discover their unique blend of spiritual gifts, personal style, and ministry passion. The participants are also taught the biblical nature and purpose of the church as the body of Christ and the unique importance of each member's contribution. The *Network Revised* material was developed by Bruce Bugbee and Don Cousins of Willow Creek Community Church to motivate people to discover, connect, and apply their unique blend of passion, gifts, and style to specific ministry opportunities. Over 800,000 people have gone through *Network* training.

Network Revised works with any size group, from small groups of 4–12 to large groups of 15 to 150 or more. *Network Revised* can be presented successfully in these different formats: 1. Three sessions of two hours each 2. Six sessions of 50 minutes each 3. One-, two-, or three-day retreats 4. The one that works best for your church!

Summary of revisions:
- Now six sessions
- Revisions allow for more complete self-understanding (Servant Profile) and ministry placement.
- Session on passion now includes a list of "Passion Categories" for easier identification and database retrieval
- Revised video vignettes (4) include ethnic diversity
- DVD segment for each of the six sessions
- Overheads reformatted, creating a PowerPoint presentation for the six sessions on a CD-ROM
- User's Guide and Consultant's Guide now on CD-ROM

The *Network Revised* Kit includes:
- Leader's Guide
- Participant's Guide
- DVD with drama vignettes, vision and coaching material
- CD-ROM includes PowerPoint materials for leaders, users, and consultants, as well as 400 ministry position descriptions

Curriculum Kit: 0-310-25793-X
Leader's Guide: 0-310-25794-8
Participant's Guide: 0-310-25795-6
DVD: 0-310-25796-4
PowerPoint® CD: 0-310-25797-2

What You Do Best in the Body of Christ

Discover Your Spiritual Gifts, Personal Style, and God-Given Passion

Bruce L. Bugbee

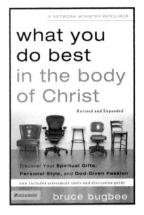

Have you found fulfillment in life? Can you say your ministry is a fruitful one? God has created you to be both fulfilled and fruitful in a meaningful place of ministry. You can discover your God-given design and the role he created for you in and through the local church. In *What You Do Best*, Bruce Bugbee helps you identify your God-given passion, spiritual gifts, and personal style. And he shows how together they point to your unique role and purpose in the body of Christ. Drawing from biblical principles, *What You Do Best* provides proven tools and a conversational approach that will guide you to a greater fulfillment of God's will for your life. You'll discover: Your God-given passion indicates where you should serve—Your God-given spiritual gifts indicate what you should do—Your God-given personal style indicates how you should serve. Together, they indicate what you do best. You'll find plenty of helpful charts and self-assessments, plus insights into the fallacies and pitfalls that can hinder your effectiveness. "You are needed in the church," says Bruce Bugbee, "not because there are slots to fill, but because in and through your ministry, God's grace is released and his purposes are fulfilled." Start learning today what God wants you to do, and experience more enthusiasm, greater joy, and real significance in your life and ministry.

This expanded edition includes discussion questions and fills the need for small groups who are unable, or whose church is unwilling, to implement the value of gifts-based ministry throughout the church.

Softcover: 0-310-25735-2

Pick up a copy today at your favorite bookstore!

ZONDERVAN™
GRAND RAPIDS, MICHIGAN 49530 USA
WWW.ZONDERVAN.COM

WILLOW
Willow Creek Resources

Discover Your Spiritual Gifts the Network Way

Bruce L. Bugbee

This is a small booklet containing five assessments in the areas of traits, observations, experiences, convictions, and ministry fit to help people understand their spiritual giftedness. This tool offers a totally unique resource for identifying a person's spiritual gifts through several perspectives or approaches. People who take a one-dimensional assessment often wonder how accurate it really is. When they are able to take multiple assessments indicating some common conclusions, it increases their confidence and motivation to serve accordingly. This tool has the opportunity to set a new standard for gifts-identification, just as *Network* has with the Servant Profile (passion, gifts, style) identification, consultation, and placement process.

Softcover: 0-310-25746-8

Look for Discover Your Spiritual Gifts the Network Way *at your local Christian bookstore.*

GRAND RAPIDS, MICHIGAN 49530 USA

WWW.ZONDERVAN.COM

WILLOW

Willow Creek Resources

We want to hear from you. Please send your comments about this book to us in care of zreview@zondervan.com. Thank you.

GRAND RAPIDS, MICHIGAN 49530 USA

WWW.ZONDERVAN.COM